PREPARE YOURSELF

This non-fiction coloring book is based off the best selling

"UNEDUCATION: A RESIDENTIAL SCHOOL GRAPHIC NOVEL"

- the chilling chronicles of a family's exploitation in the

mandatory residential/boarding school system.

The UNeducation series is used in schools, universities, corrections

centers, addictions facilities, youth groups and healing

initiatives throughout North America - and beyond.

Due to popular demand, it's now available as a coloring book

... A COLORING EXPERIENCE UNLIKE ANYTHING YOU'VE SEEN

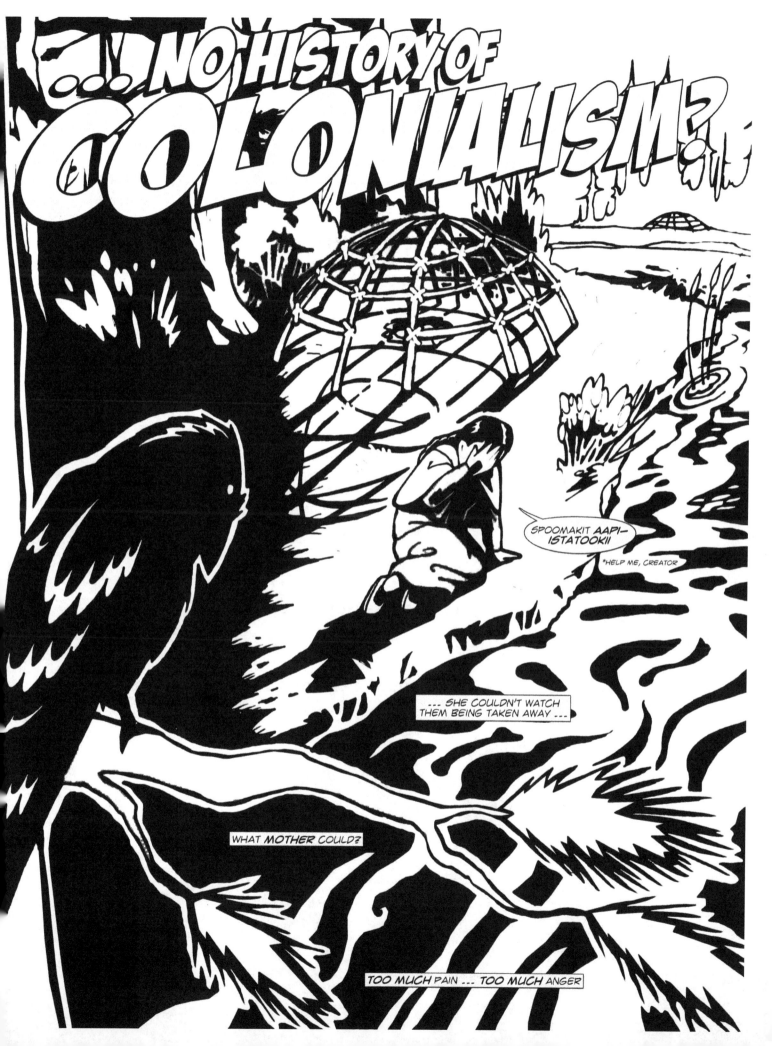

YOUR FIRST DAY

you line up with all the other kids

you look for your mom

you wonder where she is

your dad reassures you

your dad weeps ... for more reasons than you realize

you listen to the endless rules

you wonder if you'll remember them all

you're kinda scared

you're overwhelmed by the size of the residential school

you head down the stairs ... angry ladies with scissors await

your long hair is reduced to stubble

you wonder why this is

you wonder if it can get any worse

your eyes burn from the lye powder

you run screaming

your friends are screaming too

you race for the horse trough to rinse

you line up for a haircut

your long hair is long gone

your clothes all match

you're given a new English name, NEVER use your old one

you're given a number, NEVER forget your number

you listen to the endless rules - boys upstairs, girls downstairs

your brother and sister try to hug, they are quickly torn apart

you're led to a jam-packed room by a frowning lady

you're 6, so you're scared

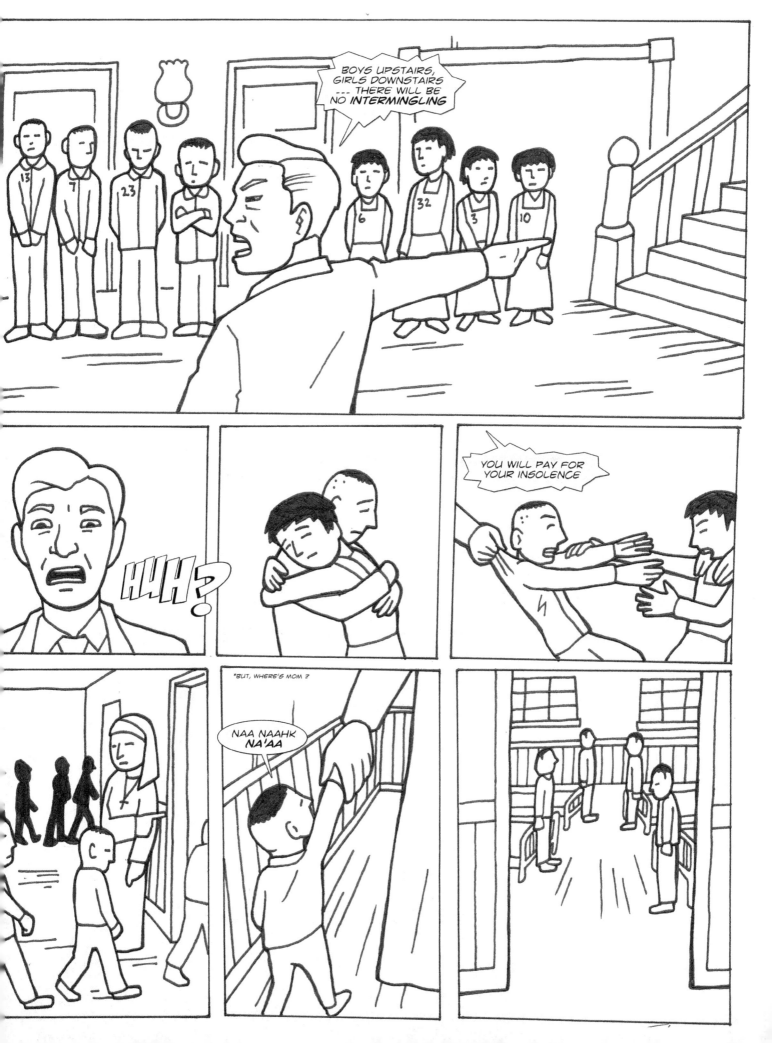

you try to run after the frowning lady, the door slams

you think to yourself "WHERE IS MY MOMMY?"

... IT'S 12 YEARS LATER

you're telling your story to a crowd of educators

you can sense the disbelief

you endure the onslaught of inevitable doubts

you sense the crowd's need for "proof"

you list out the facts ... you stream the data

you hear a curious man blurt out *"to kill the indian in the child!"*

you hear a misinformed lady yell "history is brutal, get over it!"

you explain how families weren't allowed to parent their own children

you explain how this went on for generation after generation

you sense the crowd still does not understand

you return to your family's story ...

ALL YOUR KIDS ARE GONE

you tell yourself "enough is enough"

you race towards the residential school

you know you'll get them back this time

you finally find a ride, it's a really long drive

you can almost hear your children

your heart is racing, just a few steps more

you gently knock on the huge locked door

"*you don't belong here!*", an anonymous voice yells

you gently kick the huge locked door

"*you give my children back!*"

you try to pry open the huge locked door

"you can't keep my chidren from me!"

you try to knock down the huge locked door

"you give me back my babies!"

you feel the police pull you away

"mama's here!"

you struggle and scream, but, it's just no use

you beg for help ... who will listen?

your children are inside, wondering, "how come mama never comes for us?"

your children feel abandoned

your children feel alone

your children don't understand

your children carry this into their adult years

you're 8 years old

you're running through a field ... it's 2am

you look ahead and see a glimmering town in the distance

your twin brother is tightly gripping your hand

you wonder if you'll ever make it

you see flashlights searching

you hear dogs barking

you hide then move, hide then move

you're shivering behind a propane tank, *"what do we do now?"*

you huddle with your brother for extra warmth

you have hope, but, hope is not a plan

you spot your uncle's truck

you happily race over and jump in

you're so excited, you're so happy - *"we're going home!"*

your uncle is surprised, he takes you out for chinese buffet

you talk about home, you talk about family

you talk about life, you talk about school

your uncle says *"I have to take you back!"*

you don't want to go back

you beg to stay with him, your uncle has no choice

your uncle cries as he hands you back to the school

your uncle tries to talk, but, is interrputed

"LEAVE HERE NOW, YOU KNOW THE LAW!"

you're 10 years old

you're still not used to residential school life - will you ever be?

you're in class, the teacher is gone, everyone is goofing off

you hardly speak English, you've been warned not to speak your language

you watch the teacher inspect the class, make faces as she walks by

you don't notice the teacher turn around and catch you

you're startled, you blurt out *"oki niksookwa"* (how you doing?)

your head slams hard into your desk, it happens twice

your head is spinning, you see bloody notebook pages

you crouch into ball, you feel countless kicks to your ribs

you hear over and over *"SPEAK ENGLISH, SPEAK ENGLISH!"*

your brother tries to help, he's dragged off into the darkness

you never speak your own language again

you're a teenager

you're happy the residential schools have finally closed down

you barely made it out with your sanity intact

you're ready for the world to embrace you

you're ready for a new school, everything will be alright now

you arrive, everyone is taunting you - parents, public, media

you run inside, everyone is bullying you - students, teachers, staff

you head home, everyone is profiling you - police, busdrivers, adults

you make it home

you're finally safe - until tomorrow

you deal with this everyday

you wonder if you'll ever be equal

this story's through

... here's a sneak peek at part two

see if you can figure out the story

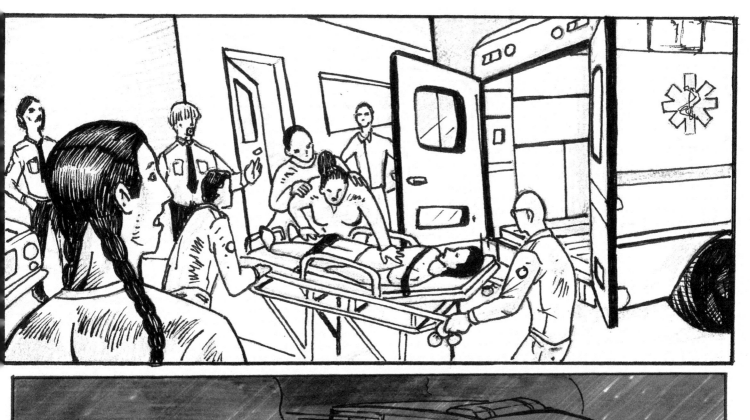

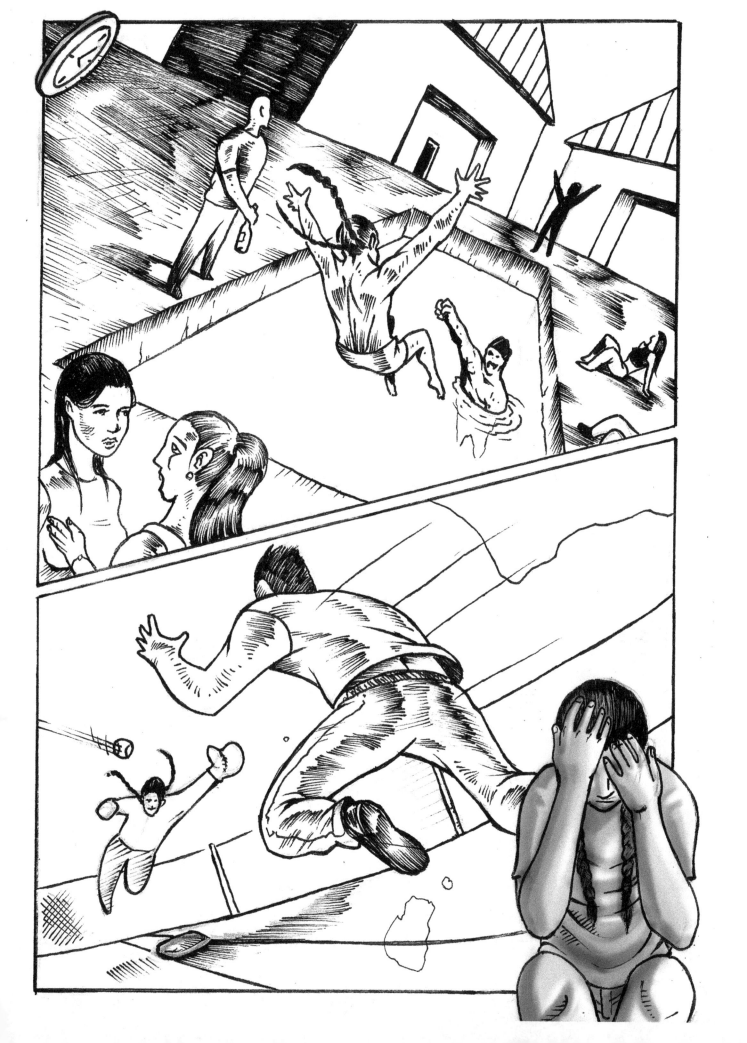

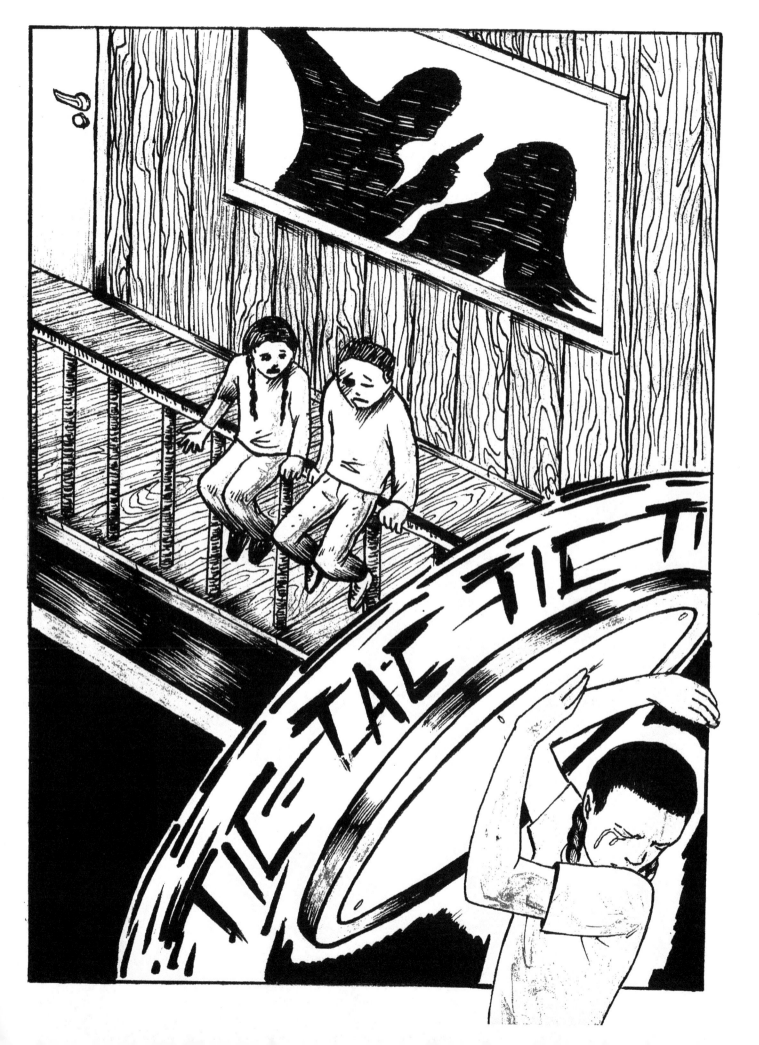

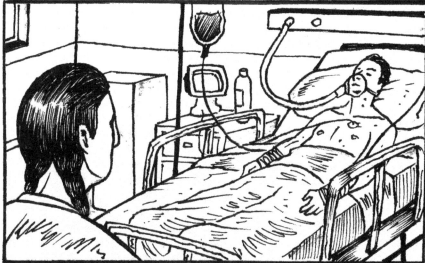
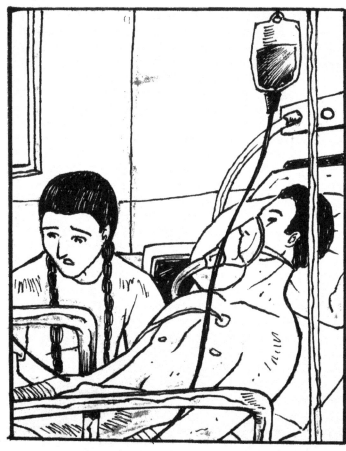
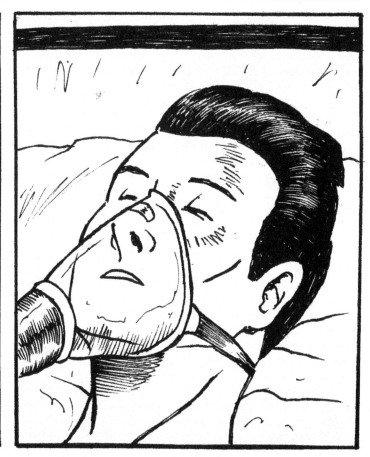

CPSIA information can be obtained
at www.ICGtesting.com
Printed in the USA
LVHW051542150721
692810LV00008B/486